TO MY SIGNIFICANT

OTTER

TO MY SIGNIFICANT OTTER

An Hachette UK Company
www.hachette.co.uk

Summersdale Publishers Ltd
Part of Octopus Publishing Group Limited
Carmelite House
50 Victoria Embankment
LONDON
EC4Y 0DZ
UK

www.summersdale.com

Printed and bound in China

ISBN: 978-1-78783-228-2

Substantial discounts on bulk quantities of Summersdale books are available to corporations, professional associations, and other organizations. For details contact general enquiries: telephone: +44 (0) 1243 771107 or email: enquiries@summersdale.com.

To...

From......................................

I WALLABY

YOUR LOVER!

LOVE
RECOGNIZES
NO BARRIERS.
IT JUMPS HURDLES,
LEAPS FENCES,
PENETRATES WALLS
TO ARRIVE AT
ITS DESTINATION
FULL OF HOPE.

Maya Angelou

THERE ARE **ALL KINDS OF LOVE** IN THIS WORLD, BUT NEVER THE SAME LOVE TWICE.

F. Scott Fitzgerald

Souls tend
to go back to
who feels like
HOME.

N. R. Hart

LOVE IS NOT CONSOLATION. IT IS LIGHT.

Simone Weil

The one thing we can never get enough of is

LOVE.

Henry Miller

YOU'RE JUST MY

PUP OF TEA

The

SOUND
OF A KISS

is not so loud as that
of a cannon, but its
echo lasts a great
deal longer.

Oliver Wendell Holmes, Sr.

YOU KNOW YOU'RE
IN LOVE WHEN YOU CAN'T
FALL ASLEEP BECAUSE
**REALITY IS FINALLY BETTER
THAN YOUR DREAMS.**

Anonymous

LET'S BE SEAL-Y

TOGETHER

Anyone can
be passionate,
but it takes

REAL
LOVERS

to be silly.

Rose Franken

A LIFE WITHOUT **LOVE** IS LIKE A YEAR WITHOUT SUMMER.

Swedish proverb

I KISSED A
LOT OF FROGS
BEFORE I FOUND
MY PRINCE.

Joan Collins

I FIND YOU

RIBBITING

I LOVE YOU

– I am at rest
with you – I have
come home.

Dorothy L. Sayers

LOVE, LIKE A RIVER, WILL CUT A NEW PATH WHENEVER IT MEETS AN OBSTACLE.

Crystal Middlemas

I'M NOT LION

WHEN I SAY
THAT I ADORE YOU

HAPPINESS IS LIKE A KISS. YOU MUST SHARE IT TO ENJOY IT.

Bernard Meltzer

YOUR WORDS
ARE MY FOOD,
YOUR BREATH MY
WINE. **YOU ARE
EVERYTHING
TO ME.**

Sarah Bernhardt

LOVE
PLANTED
A ROSE,

And the world
turned sweet.

Katharine Lee Bates

YOUR HEDGEHUGS

ARE THE BEST

A HUG IS THE
PERFECT GIFT
— one size fits all
and nobody minds if
you exchange it.

Anonymous

TO BE BRAVE IS TO
LOVE SOMEONE
UNCONDITIONALLY,
WITHOUT EXPECTING
ANYTHING IN RETURN.

Madonna

I WHALE-Y

LOVE YOU

LOVE

is what makes
you smile when
you're tired.

Paulo Coelho

ALL LOVE IS SWEET, GIVEN OR RETURNED.

Percy Bysshe Shelley

LOVE ...
IT SURROUNDS
EVERY BEING AND
EXTENDS SLOWLY
TO EMBRACE ALL
THAT SHALL BE.

Kahlil Gibran

OWL ALWAYS

LOVE YOU!

The heart

THAT LOVES

is always young.

Greek proverb

WHEN YOU
LOVE SOMEONE,
YOU LOVE THE
PERSON AS THEY
ARE, AND NOT
AS YOU'D LIKE
THEM TO BE.

Leo Tolstoy

TIME IS
IRR-ELEPHANT

WHEN I'M
WITH YOU

THERE'S ONLY
ONE THING MORE
PRECIOUS THAN
OUR TIME AND
THAT'S **WHO WE
SPEND IT ON**.

Leo Christopher

IS NOT A
KISS THE VERY
**AUTOGRAPH
OF LOVE?**

Henry Theophilus Finck

I LOVE HUGGING.

I wish I was an octopus, so I could hug ten people at a time.

Drew Barrymore

I WANT TO BEE

WITH YOU
FOREVER

Sometimes
THE HEART
sees what
is invisible to
the eye.

H. Jackson Brown, Jr.

WHATEVER OUR
SOULS ARE MADE
OF, HIS AND MINE
ARE **THE SAME**.

Emily Brontë

SOUND THE
A-LLAMA

BECAUSE YOU'RE
SMOKIN' HOT!

I have spread
my dreams under
your feet;
Tread softly
because you
tread on
MY DREAMS.

W. B. Yeats

IF I KNOW WHAT
LOVE IS, IT IS
BECAUSE OF YOU.

Hermann Hesse

WHAT THE WORLD
REALLY NEEDS IS
MORE LOVE AND
LESS PAPERWORK.

Pearl Bailey

I'LL NEVER STOP

RAVEN
ABOUT YOU

LOVE

is like dew that falls on both nettles and lilies.

Swedish proverb

THERE IS NO HEAVEN LIKE **MUTUAL LOVE.**

George Granville

YOU'RE ONE IN A

CHAMELEON

TO LOVE DEEPLY
IN ONE DIRECTION
MAKES US MORE
LOVING IN ALL
OTHERS.

Sophie Swetchine

LET YOUR HEART MELT TOWARD ME,

JUST AS THE ICE THAT MELTS IN SPRING LEAVES NO TRACE OF ITS CHILL.

Kokinshū

LOVE

is sharing
your popcorn.

Charles M. Schulz

YOU'RE SO

EMU-SING

When you
fish for love,

BAIT WITH
YOUR HEART,
not your brain.

Mark Twain

TWO SOULS WITH
BUT A SINGLE THOUGHT,
**TWO HEARTS THAT
BEAT AS ONE.**

John Keats

YOU'RE MY

SOLE-MATE

I LOVE YOU
more than coffee,
but please don't
make me prove it.

Elizabeth Evans

MORNING WITHOUT YOU IS A DWINDLED DAWN.

Emily Dickinson

IT'S THE KIND OF KISS THAT INSPIRES STARS TO CLIMB INTO THE SKY AND **LIGHT UP THE WORLD.**

Tahereh Mafi

YOU'RE

ROAR-SOME

LOVE

is when you meet
someone who tells
you something new
about yourself.

André Breton

LOVE DOESN'T
MAKE THE WORLD
GO ROUND.
LOVE IS WHAT
**MAKES THE RIDE
WORTHWHILE.**

Franklin P. Jones

CAN WE KISS
TILL THE

COWS
COME HOME?

IT JUST SORT
OF HAPPENED,
IN THE WAY THAT
LOVE OFTEN
DOES: **NATURALLY,
INSTINCTUALLY, AND
WHOLEHEARTEDLY.**

Jodi Picoult

DO YOU KNOW HOW YOU TELL **REAL LOVE?** IT'S WHEN SOMEONE ELSE'S INTEREST TRUMPS YOUR OWN.

Brad Pitt

LOVE
makes your soul
crawl out from its
hiding place.

Zora Neale Hurston

YOU OCTOP-Y

MY HEART

I wish I could turn back the clock. I'd find you sooner and

LOVE YOU LONGER.

Anonymous

WE LOVED WITH
A LOVE THAT WAS
MORE THAN LOVE.

Edgar Allan Poe

IF YOU WANT TO BE SILLY,

TOUCAN PLAY THAT GAME

No one has measured, not even poets, how much THE HEART can hold.

Zelda Fitzgerald

IT'S ALWAYS
WRONG TO HATE,
BUT IT'S **NEVER
WRONG TO LOVE.**

Lady Gaga

LIFE AND LOVE ARE **VERY PRECIOUS** WHEN BOTH ARE IN FULL BLOOM.

Louisa May Alcott

I'M NUTS

ABOUT YOU

ROMANCE

is the glamour which turns the dust of everyday life into a golden haze.

Elinor Glyn

WE LOVE BECAUSE IT'S THE ONLY **TRUE ADVENTURE.**

Nikki Giovanni

I LOVE YOU THE MOST.

I SHIH-TZU NOT!

NOTHING IS IMPOSSIBLE FOR **PURE LOVE.**

Mahatma Gandhi

HOW DO I LOVE THEE? LET ME COUNT THE WAYS.

Elizabeth Barrett Browning

TRUE LOVE STORIES

never have endings.

Richard Bach

LET'S MONKEY

AROUND

LOVE

does not consist in gazing at each other but in looking outward together in the same direction.

Antoine de Saint-Exupéry

IF YOU HAVE ONLY ONE
SMILE IN YOU, GIVE IT TO
THE PEOPLE YOU LOVE.

Maya Angelou

YOU'RE
O-FISH-ALLY

THE BEST!

If I were to live a thousand years, I would

BELONG TO YOU

for all of them.

Michelle Hodkin

LOVE MUST BE AS MUCH A LIGHT AS A FLAME.

Henry David Thoreau

FALLING IN LOVE COULD BE ACHIEVED IN A SINGLE WORD – A GLANCE.

Ian McEwan

LOVING YOU

IS NEVER
ORCA-WARD

I ask you to pass
through life at
my side — to be
MY SECOND
SELF,
and best earthly
companion.

Charlotte Brontë

LOVE IS A
FRIENDSHIP SET
TO MUSIC.

Joseph Campbell

TO ME, YOU ARE

IM-PECK-ABLE!

I LOVE YOU WITH
SO MUCH OF MY
HEART THAT NONE
IS LEFT TO PROTEST.

William Shakespeare

WHEN YOU'RE LOVED FOR YOUR FLAWS, THAT'S WHEN YOU FEEL REALLY SAFE.

Nicole Kidman

LOVE

**betters what
is best.**

Michelangelo

I HIPPOPOTA-MISS

YOU WHEN
YOU'RE AWAY

If you

REMEMBER
ME,

then I don't
care if everyone
else forgets.

Haruki Murakami

GROW OLD
ALONG WITH ME!
THE BEST IS YET TO BE.

Robert Browning

YOU HAVE ME

HOWLING

WITH LAUGHTER

LOVE
keeps the cold out better than a cloak.

Henry Wadsworth Longfellow

I HAVE LOVED NONE BUT **YOU**.

Jane Austen

IN DREAMS AND IN LOVE, THERE ARE NO IMPOSSIBILITIES.

János Arany

TO ME, YOU ARE

PRACTICALLY
PURR-FECT

For it was not
into my ear you
whispered, but

INTO MY
HEART.

Judy Garland

LOVE IS
BEING STUPID
TOGETHER.

Paul Valéry

YOU'LL ALWAYS

BE MY
SQUEAK-HEART

LOVE IS SPACE
AND TIME
MEASURED BY
THE HEART.

Marcel Proust

I WOULD RATHER SPEND **ONE LIFETIME WITH YOU** THAN FACE ALL THE AGES OF THIS WORLD ALONE.

J. R. R. Tolkien

Love was
IN HER
HEART,
like seeds in the
earth, awaiting the
action of the sun.

Honoré de Balzac

I LOVE EWE

SO MUCH

We are
MOST ALIVE
when we're in love.

John Updike

YOU GET TO CHOOSE
WHO YOU LOVE AND
WHO YOU DECIDE TO
GIVE YOUR HEART TO.

Emma Watson

YOU'RE VERY

DEER TO ME

Love is our
TRUE
DESTINY.
We do not find the
meaning of life by
ourselves alone —
we find it with
another.

Thomas Merton

JUST IN CASE
YOU EVER
FOOLISHLY
FORGET; I'M
NEVER NOT
THINKING
OF YOU.

Virginia Woolf

PERHAPS WE ARE IN THIS WORLD TO **SEARCH FOR LOVE.**

Isabel Allende

WHEN IT COMES
TO LOVE,

WE'VE SNAIL-ED IT

Forget the
BUTTERFLIES;
I feel the whole zoo
when I'm with you.

Anonymous

I WANT TO BE
WITH YOU TILL MY
LAST PAGE.

A. R. Asher

YOU MAKE ME

ALL AFLUTTER

WHEN WE FIND
SOMEONE WHOSE
WEIRDNESS IS
COMPATIBLE WITH
OURS, WE JOIN
UP WITH THEM
AND FALL INTO
MUTUALLY SATISFYING
WEIRDNESS – AND
CALL IT LOVE –
TRUE LOVE.

Robert Fulghum

LOVE IS
FRIENDSHIP
SET ON FIRE.

Jeremy Taylor

To get the

FULL
VALUE
OF JOY

you must have
someone to
divide it with.

Mark Twain

OUR LOVE IS LIKE

A FAIRY TAIL!

All
LOVE
STORIES
are tales of
beginnings.

Meghan O'Rourke

LOVE IS AN
UNTAMED FORCE.

Paulo Coelho

I AM
TURTLE-Y

IN LOVE
WITH YOU

Love is an

IRRESISTIBLE
DESIRE

to be irresistibly
desired.

Robert Frost

LOVE, AND DO WHAT THOU WILT.

Augustine of Hippo

TOGETHER,
WE SOAR.

Celeste Bradley

YOU GIVE
MY LIFE

PORPOISE!

LOVE
is quivering
happiness.

Kahlil Gibran

I HAVE BEEN
**LOVING YOU
A LITTLE MORE**
EVERY MINUTE
SINCE THIS
MORNING.

Victor Hugo

LOOKING

FOXY

YOU ARE MY
HEART, MY LIFE,
MY ONE AND
ONLY THOUGHT.

Arthur Conan Doyle

THERE'S NO BAD CONSEQUENCE TO LOVING FULLY, WITH **ALL YOUR HEART.**

Reese Witherspoon

LOVE IS
COMPOSED
of a single
soul inhabiting
two bodies.

Aristotle

THERE'S NO
REASON TO BE

MELAN-COLLIE
WHEN YOU'RE
AROUND

Where love
is concerned,
too much is
NOT EVEN
ENOUGH.

Pierre Beaumarchais

TO LOVE AND BE LOVED
IS TO FEEL THE SUN
FROM BOTH SIDES.

David Viscott

YOU'RE

DINO-MITE

The best
thing to hold
on to in life is

EACH
OTHER.

Audrey Hepburn

WE ARE ASLEEP
UNTIL **WE FALL
IN LOVE.**

Leo Tolstoy

I SEEM TO HAVE LOVED YOU IN **NUMBERLESS FORMS, NUMBERLESS TIMES** ... IN LIFE AFTER LIFE, IN AGE AFTER AGE FOREVER.

Rabindranath Tagore

LET ME PANDA

TO YOUR
EVERY NEED

If the path be

BEAUTIFUL,

let us not ask

where it leads.

Anatole France

I SAW THAT YOU WERE PERFECT, AND SO **I LOVED YOU**. THEN I SAW THAT YOU WERE NOT PERFECT, AND **I LOVED YOU EVEN MORE**.

Angelita Lim

LET'S
TAKE THE

SLOTH LANE
TOGETHER

WHEN WE ARE IN LOVE WE SEEM TO OURSELVES QUITE DIFFERENT FROM WHAT WE WERE BEFORE.

Blaise Pascal

SOUL MEETS SOUL ON **LOVERS' LIPS.**

Percy Bysshe Shelley

Lovers don't meet
somewhere along
the way. They're
in one another's souls
FROM THE
BEGINNING.

Rumi

YOU'RE THE

BEAR-Y BEST

BEING DEEPLY
LOVED BY
SOMEONE
gives you
strength, while
LOVING SOMEONE
DEEPLY
gives you courage.

Anonymous

WHEN YOU LOVE
SOMEONE, ALL YOUR
SAVED-UP WISHES
START COMING OUT.

Elizabeth Bowen

I LOVE
CHINCHILL-IN'

WITH YOU

We come to love not by finding a perfect person, but by learning to see AN IMPERFECT PERSON perfectly.

Sam Keen

IN ALL THE WORLD
THERE IS NO
HEART FOR ME
LIKE YOURS.

Maya Angelou

LOVE'S TOO PRECIOUS TO BE LOST, A LITTLE GRAIN SHALL NOT BE SPILT.

Alfred, Lord Tennyson

YOU'RE

KOALA-TY

LOVE KNOWS NOT
DISTANCE; IT HATH
NO CONTINENT;
**ITS EYES ARE FOR
THE STARS.**

Gilbert Parker

YOU ARE MY SIGNIFICANT

OTTER!

If you're interested in finding out more about our books,
find us on Facebook at **Summersdale Publishers**
and follow us on Twitter at **@Summersdale**.

www.summersdale.com